# CONTENTS

## *Acknowledgements*

The author and publishers wish to acknowledge, with thanks, the following photographic sources:

Bettmann Archive pp6 bottom, 8, 9, 12, 17 left, 20, 26, 30 bottom left, 31 left, 34, 37, 43, 44 top, 45, 46, 48; Hulton Picture Company/Bettmann pp5, 6 top and bottom, 25 bottom, 31 right, 35 bottom, 39, 49 top and bottom, 52; Magnum pp23 (photograph Bruce Davidson), 25 top (photograph Burt Glinn), 28, 44 bottom (photographs Eve Arnold), 30 top, 35 top, 36 top and bottom, 40 (photographs Bruce Davidson), 57, 58, 59 (photographs Leonard Freed), 60 (photograph Alex Webb), 61 (photograph Eli Reed); Popperfoto pp17 right, 29, 42, 53, 54, 56.

The author and publishers wish to thank the following who have kindly given permission for the use of copyright material:

The Observer Ltd. for 'Blacks in Top Job Frightens the Democrats', 29th Jan. 1989. Copyright © 1989 *The Observer*; W. J. Weatherby for 'The Growing Silence of Black Voters', October, 1988, *The Guardian*.

Every effort has been made to trace all the copyright holders, but if any have been inadvertently overlooked the publishers will be pleased to make the necessary arrangements at the first opportunity.

# PREFACE

The study of history is exciting, whether in a good story well told, a mystery solved by the judicious unravelling of clues, or a study of the men, women and children whose fears and ambitions, successes and tragedies make up the collective memory of mankind.

This series aims to reveal this excitement to pupils through a set of topic books on important historical subjects from the Middle Ages to the present day. Each book contains four main elements: a narrative and descriptive text, lively and relevant illustrations, extracts of contemporary evidence, and questions for further thought and work. Involvement in these elements should provide an adventure which will bring the past to life in the imagination of the pupil.

Each book is also designed to develop the knowledge, skills and concepts so essential to a pupil's growth. It provides a wide, varying introduction to the evidence available on each topic. In handling this evidence, pupils will increase their understanding of basic historical concepts such as causation and change, as well as of more advanced ideas such as revolution and democracy. In addition, their use of basic study skills will be complemented by more sophisticated historical skills such as the detection of bias and the formulation of opinion.

The intended audience for the series is pupils of eleven to sixteen years; it is expected that the earlier topics will be introduced in the first three years of secondary school, while the nineteenth and twentieth century topics are directed towards first examinations.

# 1 BLACK AMERICANS IN WAR

## Race riot

On a hot summer evening in June 1943 in Detroit, Michigan, a quarrel broke out between two motorists – one was white and the other was black. False rumours spread and rioting began. For three days blacks and whites fought one another. Thirty-five people were killed, over 600 were injured and two million dollars' worth of property was destroyed before the US Army was called in to help local police restore order.

The Detroit riot was only one of a number of race riots during the war, but it was the worst. Like many other northern and western cities, Detroit – 'Motor City' – had attracted huge numbers of people in search of work in flourishing war industries; nearly 500 000 people crowded into the city between 1940 and 1943. Fifty thousand of the new arrivals were blacks, mainly from the farms of the South, swelling the black population of Detroit to 200 000. Hopes of high wages, decent housing and a better life were dashed. They were packed into two areas of the city, where they lived in slum conditions: black 'ghettos' created by white people's opposition to having black neighbours. They were usually given the worst-paid jobs, and even skilled black workers were denied jobs when they competed with white workers. Sometimes employers used cheap black labour to break strikes and this added to racial tension. As the huge population increase put a strain on housing, schools and transport facilities, the blacks, so long regarded by many whites as inferior, became a convenient group to blame for the problems of the city. Of the 35 killed in the Detroit riot, 29 were black.

*Soldiers maintain order: Detroit riot, 1943.*

There were also riots in Harlem, New York, in 1943. Why do you think the store owner put these signs up?

belligerency: violent, war-like behaviour

Detroit, 1943.

*Using the evidence: two views of the Detroit riot*

A  From the official report:

(i) Some incidents leading to the riot
*The crowd of Negroes...had continued in the meantime to the bridge...the Byndon girl [colored] pushed against a [white] girl. The Negress says Margaret Hart called her a 'black bitch'....Hart denies the statement...the colored boys with the Negress attacked Miss Hart, knocking her down and kicking her....*

*But the rioting was started by an episode which occurred at the Forest club...in the heart of the Negro section some five miles from Belle Island...automobiles operated by whites were opened by the Negro mob, the whites taken from behind the wheel...a white motorcyclist was struck by a stone....*

(ii) Where responsibility lay
*What particular factor is responsible for the uncontrolled belligerency prevalent in certain white and Negro groups in Detroit? Where have these young hoodlums been told they have a licence to lawlessness in 'their struggle to secure racial equality'? Who constantly beats the drums of racial prejudice...who charges that all law enforcement agencies are anti-Negro, brutal and vicious in the handling of Negroes? The Negro press, of course.*

The Dowling Report to the Governor of Michigan, 1943

B *For years preceding the riot, there had been mob attacks on the homes of Negroes outside the so-called Negro area...houses were attacked by mobs with no police interference. Public housing provided homes for only about 3,000 Negroes. Negroes were excluded from all other such housing, erected through the taxation of Negro as well as white Americans....distrust of the police remained. When the riot broke out, this suspicion of the police by Negroes was more than justified when 29 of the 35 killed were Negroes, 17 of them shot by the police and a number of these shot in the back...photographs [in the newspapers] show the faces of 800 to 1,000 white rioters engaged in assaulting, killing, kicking or otherwise violating the law against the persons of Negroes...but as of the date of writing this report, few, if any of them, have been arrested.*
Walter White, Secretary of the National Association for the Advancement of Colored People (NAACP), 1943

1 What, according to source **A**, were (i) the immediate causes and (ii) the long-term causes of the Detroit riot?

2 What does Walter White think were the main causes of the riot?

3 Compare sources **A** and **B**, pointing out how they differ in dealing with the causes of the riot.

4 As historical evidence, in what ways could these sources be said to be biased?

5 After reading about the riot and then considering these sources, write a short paragraph giving your verdict on why it happened.

Many Americans had hoped that the war would bring about unity in a common cause and an end to racial division. White American leaders had stressed that the war was being fought for freedom and democracy, and, particularly in the case of Nazi Germany, against racialism — the belief in the superiority of one race over another. Black leaders were quick to point out the contrast between these war aims and the refusal of many employers to give black workers equal job opportunities and equal pay in the war industries.

An even more startling contrast existed at the heart of the war effort: the segregation of black and white servicemen into separate units in the armed forces, when the blacks were allowed to serve at all. At first, the Navy only accepted blacks as 'messmen', in effect servants, and the Marines and Air Corps accepted none at all. The Army took a percentage of blacks roughly equal to their percentage

*A black army unit, 1942. Only the officers were white.*

in the population but kept them rigidly segregated and, at first, away from combat duties. Gradually more blacks were allowed into fighting units, but their treatment created a feeling of outrage amongst men fighting a war against racialism. Fighting, even gun battles, occurred at American army bases during the war.

> *Added to the rebuffs from industry and the armed services were a hundred others. Negroes eager to contribute to the Red Cross blood programme were turned away. Despite the fact that white and negro blood is biologically the same, the Army decided that 'it is not deemed advisable to collect and mix the blood...for later administration to the armed forces'.*
>
> R.H. Dalfiume: *Desegregation of the US Armed Forces*, 1969

Stung by such insults, some black Americans rejected a 'white man's war'. Most, however, were willing to help on condition that something was done to end racialism in America. A black newspaper launched the 'Double V' campaign: 'Victory over our enemies at home and victory over our enemies on the battlefields abroad.' According to one black writer: 'The Negro was no longer willing to accept discrimination without protest.'

In 1941 a black trade union leader, A. Philip Randolph, called for a march of 10 000 blacks on the capital, to end discrimination in defence industries and the armed forces. Support for the March on Washington Movement (MOWM) mushroomed and it seemed likely the numbers would reach 100 000 by 1 July, the appointed day. President Franklin Roosevelt was anxious to avoid a confrontation with black protesters in the capital, so he arranged to meet Randolph

*A. Philip Randolph, black trade union leader and organiser of the March on Washington Movement, addresses an FEPC rally.*

at the White House. Randolph agreed to call off the march in return for the setting up of a Fair Employment Practices Committee (FEPC) by the President. The results of the deal were a great disappointment to the blacks. Richard Polenberg, an historian, wrote later that 'nothing was said about integrating the armed forces or equipping the FEPC with power to enforce its orders'. Randolph's movement was important, however, because it showed that there was mass black support for protest. In this way it was a forerunner of the mass civil rights movements of the 1950s and 1960s.

*Using the evidence: the blacks in war*

A  *Leadership is not imbedded in the Negro race yet and to try to make Negroes commissioned officers to lead men into battle – colored men – is only to work disaster to both. Colored troops do very well under white officers but every time we try to lift them a little beyond where they can go, disaster follows...we are preparing to give the Negroes a fair shot in every service...even to aviation where I doubt very much if they will not produce disaster...I hope for heaven's sake they won't mix the white and colored troops together.*
    Diary entry written by Henry Stimson, Secretary of War, 30 September 1940

B  *It so happens that a relatively large percentage of the Negroes in the Army have fallen within the lower educational classifications, and many of the Negro units accordingly have been unable to master efficiently the techniques of modern weapons.*
    Henry Stimson, letter to a Congressman, 19 February 1944

C  *The problem outlined by Stimson arose because... whereas whites from poor educational backgrounds were scattered throughout the army, blacks with the same deficiencies were concentrated in all-black units.*
    N.A. Wynn: *The Afro-American and the Second World War*, 1976

F.D.R.:  President Franklin D. Roosevelt
MP:  military policeman

D  *They say this is a war
For freedom over there.
Say, Mr F.D.R.,
How 'bout some freedom here?
T'was a Fort Bragg MP shot him down
One evening when he was leaving town.*
    'Ballad of Ned Turman', *Pittsburgh Courier*, 1942

**E** *...stories of attacks upon Negro soldiers, continued segregation and discrimination in the armed forces of the United States, the anti-Negro statements of people like the Governor of Georgia...are grist to the mill of the Tokyo and Berlin radios who cite these outrages to the one billion brown, yellow and black peoples of the Pacific and Africa.*

Walter White, Secretary of the NAACP, 1943

**F** *[Black American soldiers posted to England gained their] first experience in being treated as normal human beings and friends by white people.*

Walter White: *A Rising Wind*, 1945

**G** *The treatment accorded the Negro during the Second World War marks for me a turning point in the Negro's relation to America. To put it briefly...a certain hope died, a certain respect for White Americans faded....you must put yourself in the skin of a man who is wearing the uniform of his country, is a candidate for death in its defence, and who is called a 'nigger' by his comrades-in-arms and his officers; who is almost always given the hardest, ugliest, most menial work to do; who knows that the white GI has informed the Europeans that he is sub-human...who does not drink in the same bars that white soldiers drink in; who watches German prisoners of war being treated by Americans with more human dignity than he has ever received at their hands....*

James Baldwin: *The Fire Next Time*, 1963

*GI:* popular name given to American servicemen (from the term Government Issue)

1   Why do you think that the views of Henry Stimson would be seen as particularly important and particularly insulting by black Americans?

2   Why, according to source **C**, did black servicemen appear to be less efficient than white servicemen?

3   Ned Turman, a black soldier, was shot outside his camp at Fort Bragg, North Carolina. What do you think the ballad (source **D**) is saying to its readers?

4   Why does Walter White think that the treatment of black people in the United States (source **E**) is damaging the American war effort?

5   Look again at sources **F** and **G**, then write a letter home from a black serviceman stationed in England during the war, stating his feelings about serving abroad in an all-black army unit.

# 2  BEING BLACK IN POST-WAR AMERICA

## The segregated South

James Baldwin, an outstanding black writer, summed up the feelings of the returning black servicemen in these words:

> *Home! The very word begins to have a despairing...ring. You must consider what happens to this citizen, after all he has endured, when he returns home: search, in his shoes, for a job, for a place to live; ride, in his skin, on segregated buses; see, with his eyes, the signs saying 'White' and 'Colored', and especially the signs that say 'White Ladies' and 'Colored Women'.*
>
> James Baldwin: *The Fire Next Time*, 1963

Four years before Baldwin wrote those words, a white writer, John Howard Griffin, decided to do just what Baldwin suggested: to find out what life was like in a black man's skin. Having undergone medical treatment to darken his skin, he travelled through the Deep South, regarded as the most racially prejudiced area of the United States. His book, *Black Like Me*, is a vivid account of the fears and humiliations experienced by those who belong to a race automatically regarded as inferior by white people. Even everyday things, which a white person takes for granted, became, for the 'black' Griffin, major problems:

*drugstore:* chemist's and general goods shop with counter (the soda fountain) selling drinks, ice cream and light refreshments

> *...an important part of my daily life was spent searching for...a place to eat, or somewhere to find a drink of water, a rest room, somewhere to wash my hands. More than once I walked into a drugstore where a Negro can buy cigarettes or anything else except soda fountain service. I asked politely where I might find a glass of water. Though they had water not three yards away, they carefully directed me to the nearest Negro café....I learned to eat a great deal when it was available...in many sparsely settled areas, Negro cafés do not exist.*
>
> J.H. Griffin: *Black Like Me*, 1962

| Black population of the United States | | | |
|---|---|---|---|
| Year | Total population | Total black population | Percentage of black people |
| 1940 | 131 000 000 | 12 000 000 | 9.8 |
| 1950 | 150 000 000 | 15 000 000 | 10.0 |
| 1960 | 179 000 000 | 19 000 000 | 10.5 |
| 1970 | 203 000 000 | 22 000 000 | 11.0 |
| 1980 | 226 000 000 | 26 000 000 | 11.7 |

*Segregation in practice: separate waiting rooms.*

The problems which Griffin encountered were the result of a huge body of laws passed by the southern states with the deliberate intention of separating whites and blacks in every aspect of life. This had been achieved by slavery until it was abolished during the American Civil War (1861−5). By the early twentieth century, every southern state had found a new way to control the black population − the 'Jim Crow' laws, named after a comic stage character played by a white man 'blacked up'. These laws ordered separate waiting rooms at bus and railway stations, separate seating on buses, separate railway carriages, separate seats in theatres and cinemas, separate schools, separate churches, separate wards in hospitals − the list was endless. At the same time, the majority of blacks were prevented from voting and so had no political power with which they could challenge these laws. Ingenious ways were found to take away the blacks' right to vote and to get round the American Constitution which stated:

*The right of citizens to vote shall not be denied...by any state on account of race, color, or previous condition of servitude.*

In many states you could only vote if you paid a poll tax. Often, blacks were too poor to do so, but if they did manage to pay, they then faced so-called literacy tests'. They were asked questions that were absurdly difficult, or simply absurd:

*A black man in Mississippi was disqualified for failing to answer the question: How many bubbles are there in a bar of soap?*
R. Polenberg: *One Nation Divisible*, 1980

It was not just laws which kept the blacks 'in their place'. There were daily reminders of their inferiority. Never called 'Mister', a black man was addressed by his first name or, regardless of age, as 'boy'; women were called 'auntie' or 'girl'. Blacks were always expected to go to the back door of a white person's house. Behind the framework of laws and customs lay an atmosphere of intimidation and fear: white juries would rarely punish white people accused of violence towards blacks, and the police would harass blacks on the thinnest evidence of wrongdoing. Intimidation grew when black people began to demand equal rights in the 1950s. White organisations such as the notorious Ku Klux Klan, set up to terrorise the freed slaves after the Civil War, reappeared, and new groups, claiming to use only lawful methods of action, sprang into existence under the name of White Citizens Councils. The dreadful practice of lynching may have died away, but the story of the civil rights years was littered with cases of death and destruction of property among blacks.

---

*Using the evidence: a bus journey in Georgia*

*As always, we Negroes sat at the rear. At one of the stops, two white women boarded and could find no place to sit. No gallant Southern white man arose to offer them a place in the 'white section'. The driver called back and asked the young Negro man and the middle-aged Negro woman to sit together so the white women could have one of the seats. Both ignored the request. We felt the tension mount as the whites craned to stare back at us.*

*A red-headed white man stood up...and called out: 'Didn't you hear the driver? Move out, man.'*

*'They're welcome to sit here,' the Negro said quietly, indicating the empty seat beside him and the one beside the woman across the aisle. The driver looked dumbfounded and then dismayed. He walked...to the rear and...said: 'They don't want to sit with you people, don't you know that?' ...the young Negro said no more. He gazed out of the window.*

*The red-head bristled: 'Do you want me to slap these two jigaboos out of their seats?' he asked the driver.*

*'No — for God's sake — please — no rough stuff,' the driver pleaded. One of the white women looked towards us apologetically.... 'It's alright,' she said...asking the driver and the man to end their attempts to get her a seat.*

*The red-head flexed his muscles...glaring back at us. A young teenager...sniggered: 'Man, he was going to slap that nigger.' At Atlanta station we waited for the whites to get off...a large, middle-aged man hesitated...he bent over to speak to the young Negro.... 'I just wanted to tell you that before he slapped you, he'd have had to slap me first...I just wanted you to know — I was on your side, boy.'*

J.H. Griffin: *Black Like Me*, 1962

1  Write a sentence or two describing how each of the following felt about the incident recounted by Griffin:
   a) the bus driver;
   b) the white woman looking for a seat;
   c) the red-haired man;
   d) the white teenager;
   e) the young Negro man;
   f) the other Negro passengers;
   g) the large, middle-aged white man.

2  Use the passage to explain:
   a) the meaning of the 'Jim Crow' laws;
   b) the ways in which words were used to make blacks feel inferior;
   c) why blacks felt they were surrounded by an 'atmosphere of intimidation and fear'.

## Segregation outside the South

At first sight the position of blacks outside the South seemed better: there were no Jim Crow laws, blacks were more likely to get justice in the courts, and, most important, they could register to vote and so exercise some political power. However, as the blacks who migrated to the northern states soon found out, segregation was not just a matter of laws:

> *They do not escape Jim Crow: they encounter another, not less deadly, variety.*

> James Baldwin, 1961

At the heart of the problem was the discrimination that blacks faced in jobs and housing. Most blacks were poor and their chances of escaping from poverty were small because of their colour. In a speech given in 1963, President Kennedy drew attention to the plight of the blacks, not just in the South but across the nation:

> *The Negro baby born in America today — regardless of the section or state in which he is born — has about one half as much chance of completing high school as a white baby born in the same place on the same day — one third as much chance of completing college — one third as much chance of becoming a professional man — twice as much chance of becoming unemployed — about one seventh as much chance of earning ten thousand dollars per year — a life expectancy which is seven years less — and the prospects of earning only half as much.*

## Using the evidence

### A Occupation by per cent of population in 1960

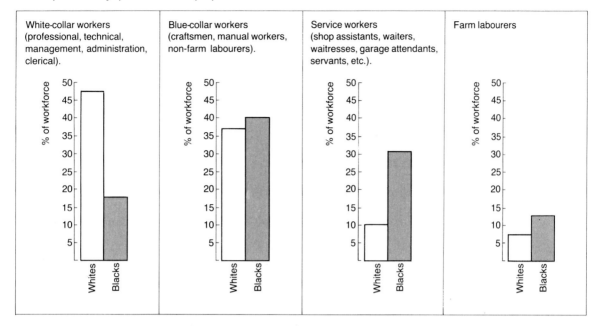

White-collar workers (professional, technical, management, administration, clerical).

Blue-collar workers (craftsmen, manual workers, non-farm labourers).

Service workers (shop assistants, waiters, waitresses, garage attendants, servants, etc.).

Farm labourers

### B Unemployment by percentage

| Year | Black | White |
|------|-------|-------|
| 1955 | 8.0 | 4.5 |
| 1960 | 10.2 | 4.9 |
| 1965 | 8.1 | 4.1 |
| 1970 | 8.2 | 4.5 |

### C Black income as a percentage of white income

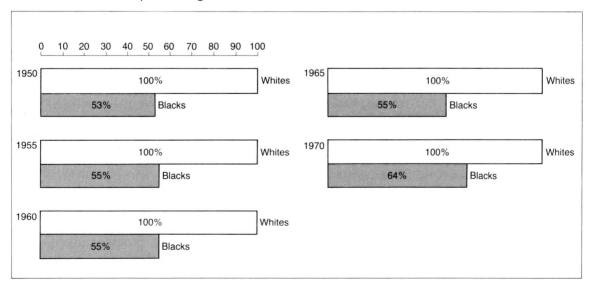

1 Examine the figures in source **A**, then make a list of the percentages of whites and blacks in each occupation.
  a) What conclusions do you draw from these figures about the general pattern of black occupations in 1960?
  b) Why do you think that blacks are in the majority in three of the categories and in the minority in the other one?

2 Examine source **B**.
  a) Blacks often said that they were 'hired last and fired first'. Does source **B** support or contradict this statement? Explain your answer.
  b) Why do you think black unemployment was higher than that of whites?

3 Do the figures in source **C** suggest that between 1950 and 1970 blacks made (a) no progress, (b) modest progress, (c) substantial progress in increasing their incomes compared to whites? Explain your answer.

For migrating blacks, the end of their journey was the city and, within the city, the black ghetto, where they joined the blacks already living there. As the blacks flooded into Harlem in New York, the South Side in Chicago or Watts in Los Angeles, so the remaining whites moved out to the 'white suburbs' if they could afford it. Dwellings were subdivided to accommodate more families who could, anyway, afford only the cheapest housing. Ghettos were overcrowded, unhealthy and a breeding ground for crime and drug trafficking. People living in them became trapped in what was called a 'cycle of poverty'. Many were unemployed. If they could get jobs, they were usually the most menial and poorly paid. Trade unions often did little for blacks and some excluded them altogether. Ghetto schools were usually poorly equipped and had low standards, so few young blacks could escape from the poverty cycle since better jobs demanded better educational qualifications. Even those who did manage to get better-paid jobs found it difficult to move out of the ghetto. Residents in white areas deliberately excluded black families:

> *Discrimination in housing is not limited to low-income blacks. Many well-known, upper-class blacks — baseball players, opera singers, popular entertainers, judges and educators — have experienced difficulty in finding housing outside the black neighborhoods of large cities.*

> A. Pinkney: *Black Americans*, 1975

In the North, as well as the South, black people of all classes could not escape the 'colour line'. In the South it was clearly visible; in the North, it was sometimes more hidden but no less real:

*debilitating:* lowering the spirits

*Racism in the non-South is a very real thing, and I join with Southern whites in denouncing Northern white people who...talk about...Mississippi and Alabama, while practising, or allowing to be practised, the most debilitating kind of discrimination in their own backyard.*

Louis Lomax: *The Negro Revolt,* 1962

## Using the evidence: life in the ghetto

A

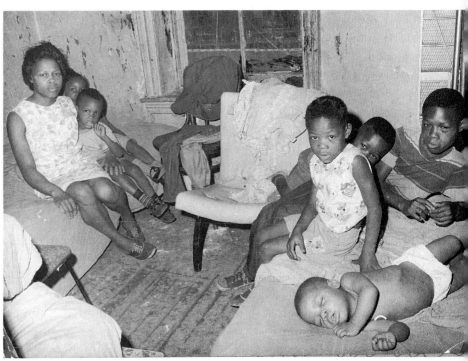

B   A description of Harlem:

*respiratory:* affecting the lungs

*The most concrete fact of the ghetto is its physical ugliness — the dirt, the filth, the neglect. The effects of unsafe, deteriorating and overcrowded housing...are well understood. The multiple use of toilet and water facilities, inadequate heating...and crowded sleeping quarters increase the rate of acute respiratory infections and infectious childhood diseases...poor electrical connections and badly lighted and unstable stairs increase the rate of home accidents. Nor is the street safer. Parks...and recreational areas are inadequate and ugly and many children play in the streets where heavy truck traffic flows...far more children are killed by cars in Harlem than in the rest of the city.*

K. Clark: *Dark Ghetto,* 1965

C   *I make $40 or $50 a day selling marijuana. You want me to go down to the garment district and push one of those trucks through the street and at the end of the week take home $40 or $50 if I am lucky? They don't have animals doing what you want me to do. There would be some society to protect animals if anybody had them pushing them damn trucks around. Go away, mister. I got to look out for myself.*

A Harlem drug dealer quoted in K. Clark's book,
*Dark Ghetto*, 1965

D   *...the final degradation the Negro must face is the image the white man has of him. White America keeps the Negro down. It forces him into a slum; it keeps him in the dirtiest and lowest-paying jobs. Having imposed this indignity, the white man [says] the ghetto reflects the 'natural' character of the Negro: lazy, shiftless, irresponsible....*

Michael Harrington: *The Other America*, 1962

1   Using sources **A** and **B**, explain briefly why living in a ghetto often leads to (a) poor health (b) high accident rates (c) mental depression and apathy.

2   Which source do you think gives the most vivid impression of life in the ghetto? Explain your answer.

3   What does source **D** tell you about white attitudes towards blacks?

4   Look again at the comments of the drug dealer (source **C**). How would (a) most white people and (b) Michael Harrington feel about these comments?

# 3 | THE CIVIL RIGHTS MOVEMENT: 1945-60

## Change at a snail's pace (1945–54)

*ideologies:* an ideology is a set of ideas

*Blacks and an increasing sector of liberal white America came out of the war with a fresh determination to uproot racist ideologies and institutions at home....*

M. Marable: *Race, Reform and Rebellion,* 1984

The blacks who had flooded into the northern cities in the 1940s possessed one important weapon with which to fight for equal rights: the vote. During the 1930s, due to Franklin Roosevelt's New Deal which promised more jobs and better wages, this vote had, by a large majority, gone to the Democratic Party. After the war Roosevelt's successor, Harry Truman, saw the importance of keeping the black vote as the revived Republican Party threatened the Democrats. In 1946 Truman set up a Commission on Civil Rights. Its report, called 'To Secure These Rights', said that 'the national government should assume leadership in our American civil rights programme'.

In the 1948 presidential election campaign, the Democrats committed themselves to such a programme. It was a risky policy because it angered the powerful southern white Democrats, some of whom switched their support to the Southern Rights candidates. But the Democrats' strategy worked. Truman won the presidency with the support of nearly 70 per cent of black voters:

*wards:* areas that cities are divided into for elections

*...in the key states of California, Illinois and Ohio, Truman obtained razor-thin majorities; [large numbers of votes] in the black wards of Los Angeles, Chicago and Cleveland spelled the difference between victory and defeat.*

R. Polenberg: *One Nation Divisible,* 1980

For the blacks, the results of the Democratic victory were, however, extremely disappointing. An effort was made to improve employment prospects for blacks in government occupations by strengthening the Fair Employment Practices Committee (see page 9). And at last segregation was ended in the armed forces, although the Army delayed action until the Korean War (1950–53) forced their hand. But this was all. Why was so little done? The answer lies mainly in the atmosphere of fear and mistrust of change created in post-war America by the Cold War, the bitter conflict with the Soviet Union. Anyone who was critical of American society, as the black civil rights leaders were bound to be, was liable to be accused of 'rocking the boat' or of being a Communist or a Communist sympathiser. The

Paul Robeson demonstrates on behalf of black people in 1950. Explain the demands made for black people on Robeson's banner. (Note: Taft Hartley was an Act restricting the rights of trade unions.)

world-famous black singer and actor, Paul Robeson, expressed the view that black people were shown more respect in the Soviet Union than in the United States. He was violently denounced for his opinions:

> ...his career went into eclipse. In Peekskill, New York, rock throwing ex-servicemen, with the connivance of the police, disrupted a concert at which he was scheduled to appear. FBI agents staked out his home and followed him wherever he went. In 1950 the State Department lifted his passport...one [Congressman] said that Robeson wanted to be 'the black Stalin among Negroes'.
>
> R. Polenberg: *One Nation Divisible*, 1980

## Using the evidence

A  *...racial segregation is the greatest single propaganda and political weapon in the hands of Russia and international communism today.*
    A. Philip Randolph, the black trade union leader, 1948

B  *[...the proposed Fair Employment Practices Commission formed part] of a communist-inspired conspiracy to undermine American unity.*
    Congressman Bryson of South Carolina, 1948

C  *What I find appalling – and really dangerous – is the American assumption that the Negro is so contented with his lot here that only the cynical agents of the Soviet Union can rouse him to protest. It is a notion that contains an insult, implying as it does that Negroes can make no move unless they are manipulated.*
    James Baldwin: *Nobody Knows My Name*, 1961

1  Why do you think Randolph says that segregation is a weapon for Russia?

2  Explain the meaning of Bryson's remark and say what you think was his attitude to civil rights.

3  What is the 'insult' to which Baldwin refers?

4  In what ways do you think the Cold War (a) helped those calling for civil rights and (b) hindered the struggle for black civil rights?

| Main black organisations involved in the struggle for civil rights ||
|---|---|
| *Name and date founded* | *Policy* |
| NAACP: National Association for the Advancement of Colored People (1909) | Promotion of civil rights through peaceful means, especially through the courts. |
| NUL: National Urban League (1911) | Equal conditions and opportunities for black workers in trade unions and employment. |
| CORE: Congress of Racial Equality (1942) | Strong pacifist aims and non-violent protest. |
| SCLC: Southern Christian Leadership Conference (1957) | Promotion of non-violent methods of protest, led by Martin Luther King. |
| SNCC: Student Non-violent Coordinating Committee (1960) | Black and white non-violent student protest; promoted sit-ins. |
| Black Muslims (1930) | Believed in black nationalism, the formation of a separate black state and self-defence against violence. |

## The pace increases (1954–60)

*The Browns, a Topeka, Kansas, Negro family, got fed up. Their daughter was a student at an inferior all-Negro school; she had been denied admission to the 'white' school...they sued for the right to send their daughter to attend the 'white' school....*

Louis Lomax: *The Negro Revolt*, 1962

The case went to the Supreme Court, the highest court in the land, and on 17 May 1954 the court made its historic decision:

*We conclude that in the field of public education the doctrine of 'separate but equal' has no place. Separate educational facilities are inherently unequal.*

Blacks, and many white liberals, rejoiced; it was the first major break in the walls of segregation. It was also a triumph for the black organisations that had been working for black civil rights, some of them for decades (see chart). However, it was only the opening shot in what turned out to be a long and often violent battle for a better deal. The court's decision to end segregation in schools had to be carried out in the face of what was bound to be fierce opposition from many southern whites. Some southern states, particularly those bordering the North, acted quickly to obey the court; others dug in their heels and defied it, even when, in 1955, the court ordered that the decision should be carried out 'with all deliberate speed'. Before the battle over the schools really got under way, the struggle against segregation moved to another issue:

*In the early hours of 1 December 1955, a bright yellow bus passed through the square in the heart of Montgomery, Alabama, and stopped....several white passengers boarded the bus, whereupon the driver asked four Negroes to stand. Three complied but Mrs Rosa Parks, 42-year-old seamstress, refused.*

Carl Rowan: *Go South to Sorrow*, 1957

Right: *Rosa Parks sits in the front of a bus in Montgomery, Alabama, in December 1956. Why did a similar scene cause an uproar a year before?*

Below: *the result of Rosa Parks' courage: black and white passengers sit side by side in Norfolk, Virginia, in 1956.*

*Martin Luther King emerged as a leader of the blacks as a result of the Montgomery bus boycott.*

*charismatic:* possessing special qualities that inspire others
*aspirations:* hopes

It was an incident just like that experienced by John Howard Griffin (see Chapter 2), but in this case the driver called the police, who arrested Mrs Parks and charged her with breaking the city's segregation laws. Three days later she was fined $10 with $4 costs. Rosa Parks was a highly respected figure in the black community and an active worker for the NAACP. Black leaders in Montgomery, aware of the outrage felt over the incident, organised a boycott of the buses. For nearly a year blacks, who made up 70 per cent of passengers, refused to ride on the buses. Instead, they walked, cycled or organised car pools to get to work. Eventually they won; the Supreme Court outlawed segregation on the Montgomery buses in November 1956. The victory in Montgomery produced a new leader for the civil rights movement: the Montgomery Improvement Association chose as its president the Rev. Martin Luther King. A 26-year-old Baptist minister from Atlanta, he had lived in Montgomery for only a year.

*[Overnight] he became the charismatic symbol of the aspirations of black people across the world.*
M. Marable: *Race, Reform and Rebellion,* 1984

Martin Luther King was a superb public speaker, one of the many black clergymen who used the skills learned in the pulpit to spread the message of the civil rights movement. Also, he had a particular message to teach, that of the Indian civil rights leader, Mahatma Gandhi:

*It was in this Gandhian emphasis on love and non-violence that I discovered the method of social reform that I had been seeking.*
M.L. King: *Stride Toward Freedom,* 1959

In 1957 King helped to form the Southern Christian Leadership Conference (SCLC) to spread the idea of non-violent protest across the South. It was a brave and difficult policy to maintain, as King quickly learned during the Montgomery campaign: in January 1956 his house was bombed. But non-violence was the tactic adopted by civil rights movements during the next ten years.

---

*Using the evidence: the tactics of non-violence*

*litigation:* bringing a case to court
*legislation:* making laws

A   *Non-violent resistance...is not meant as a substitute for litigation and legislation, which must continue. But those who adhere to the method of non-violent direct action recognise that legislation and court orders tend only to declare rights — they can never thoroughly deliver them. Only when people themselves begin to act are rights on paper given life....non-violent resistance is effective in...disarming opponents. It exposes their moral defences, weakens their morale and...works on their conscience ...non-violence also says you can struggle without hating.*

23

*We will not obey unjust laws...we will do this peacefully,
openly, cheerfully — because our aim is to persuade.*
Martin Luther King: *New York Times* magazine,
5 August 1962

B   Ray Charles, the blind black singer, wrote:

*I figured that if I was going to pick up my cross and follow
someone, it could only be a cat like King. Yet I couldn't see
me doing any marching. First, I wouldn't have known when
to duck when they started throwing beer bottles at my
head. And, secondly, I'd just defeat Martin's purpose...I
can take abuse, but if you touch me...man, that's another
story. I hit back.*

Ray Charles: *Brother Ray*, 1980

1   Why do you think Martin Luther King felt that non-violent
tactics are more effective than violent methods?

2   Why would Ray Charles not do any marching for King?

3   Whose attitude do you agree with — that of King or that of
Charles? Which of these attitudes was the most difficult to
follow and keep up?

---

While Martin Luther King called for non-violent protest, southern
white opposition to the civil rights movement became stronger and
increasingly violent:

*...all over the South the lights of reason and tolerance and moder-
ation began to go out.*
C. Vann Woodward: *Strange Career of Jim Crow*, 1974

Moderate whites were afraid to voice their opinions and politicians
found it easy to win votes by opposing any progress towards desegregation. In 1957 an incident occurred in Little Rock, Arkansas, which
showed the violence of southern opposition to school desegregation.
Just as the High School in Little Rock was about to admit its first
black children, the Arkansas Governor, Orval Faubus, ordered the
state's National Guard (part-time soldiers) to prevent the nine black
children from entering. Faubus claimed that it would not be possible
to maintain order if the black children were admitted. In fact, his
action provoked the disorder he had predicted — an angry mob of
whites turned up to witness the black children being turned away
from Central High. Two weeks later, when the court ordered that
the children should be admitted, Faubus withdrew the National
Guard and the television news reports showed the nation the ugly
scenes that developed:

*A mob of belligerent, shrieking and hysterical demonstrators forced the withdrawal today of nine Negro students...at eight o'clock some 500 persons had gathered...six black girls and three boys crossed over the school yard...they joked and chatted among themselves and carried armfuls of textbooks. The crowd let out a roar of anger...a group of girls started to shriek and wail. 'The niggers are in our school,' they howled hysterically.*

A. Lewis: *Portrait of a Decade*, 1964

At noon the nine children were smuggled out of the school through a side entrance. President Eisenhower, who had been reluctant to get involved in the issue of civil rights, was forced to act to uphold the orders of the court. He spoke of the 'disgraceful occurrence' at Little Rock and sent 1000 paratroopers to the city to ensure the law was obeyed. For a year the federal troops remained to escort the black children to school and 24 paratroopers patrolled the corridors of the school to protect the children.

*Federal troops at Little Rock High School, September 1957. When pictures like these appeared in the newspapers, how do you think Americans felt (a) in the South and (b) in the North?*

A

*Elizabeth Eckford walking through the jeering white mob on her way to Little Rock High School, September 1957.*

B  *The crowd began to follow me, calling me names...when I got in front of the school, I went up to the guard...he didn't move...when I tried to squeeze past him, he raised his bayonet. Someone started yelling, 'Lynch her, lynch her.' I tried to see a friendly face somewhere in the mob.*

Fifteen-year-old Elizabeth Eckford, one of the nine black children at Little Rock's Central High School, 1957. Quoted in A. Lewis's book, *Portrait of a Decade*, 1964

C  *One day Elizabeth [Eckford] walked into the office of the Vice Principal: red eyed, her handkerchief a damp ball in her hand, she said, 'I want to go home.' Her story was one that became too familiar during the rest of the year from all the black children...the name calling, thrown objects, trippings, shovings, kickings.*

J. Williams: *Eyes on the Prize*, 1987

D  *As for relations between the majority of white students and the nine Negroes, they are cautious and correct. A small minority of troublemakers has tried to jostle and insult the Negroes.*

*Time* magazine, October 1957

**E** Robin: *And when Elizabeth Eckford had to walk down in front of the school I was there...and I may say I was ashamed — I felt like crying.*

Kay: *Well...my parents and a lot of the other students and their parents think the Negroes aren't equal to us. But — I don't know. It seems like they are to me.*

White students at Central High, Little Rock, 1957. Quoted in A. Lewis's book, *Portrait of a Decade*, 1964

1 Look again at sources **A** and **B**, then write a short paragraph explaining the feelings of Elizabeth Eckford, arriving for her first day at Central High, Little Rock.

2 Look again at sources **C**, **D** and **E**. What conclusions do you come to about the attitudes of white students to the introduction of black students into Central High? Do you think those attitudes changed?

3 Write a brief account of life at Central High, Little Rock, in the first term of mixed black and white schooling, as it might have appeared to (a) a black student and (b) a white student.

---

The hard-won victories of Montgomery and Little Rock showed just how difficult it was for black people to achieve any advances in civil rights. In 1957 the passage through Congress of the first Civil Rights Act for 82 years revealed how limited the advances were. The Act attempted to make it easier for blacks to vote in the South by giving the federal government greater powers to investigate and put right complaints. Southern politicians found ways of avoiding its regulations and it was little more than a gesture to black people. Blacks were becoming impatient:

*One can give freedom only by setting someone free...white Americans have contented themselves with gestures that are now described as 'tokenism'. For hard example, white Americans congratulate themselves on the 1954 Supreme Court decision....they suppose in spite of a mountain of evidence to the contrary that this was proof of a change of heart.*

James Baldwin: *The Fire Next Time*, 1963

*As of June 1961, seven years after the Court's decision, 7 per cent of the South's public school Negroes were attending integrated schools.*

Louis Lomax: *The Negro Revolt*, 1962

# THE CIVIL RIGHTS MOVEMENT: 1960-65

## *The rise of non-violent direct action*

On 1 February 1960 four black students sat down in the 'whites only' section of a Woolworths lunch counter in Greensboro, North Carolina. The staff refused to serve them, but the students sat there until the store closed. The next day they returned and the newspapers

*Training for non-violent civil rights demonstrations, St. Petersburg, Florida, 1960. Explain what is happening in these photographs.*

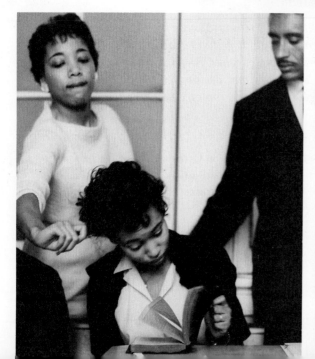

*Demonstrations in Atlanta, Georgia, 1964. Explain (a) why you think the blacks are demonstrating outside a restaurant, and (b) why the whites are marching outside a hotel and why they are dressed as they are.*

got hold of the story. The idea of non-violent protest spread rapidly across the South. There were 'stand-ins' at theatres refusing to sell tickets to blacks; 'wade-ins' at segregated swimming pools; and 'pray-ins' at 'whites only' churches. These new forms of non-violent direct action brought black and, increasingly, white students into the civil rights movement and provided a dramatic focus for the issue. Some businesses swiftly gave in and removed restrictions on blacks, but in other areas the protesters were treated violently and were arrested for 'trespassing'.

A new organisation sprang up to provide leadership for the movement: the Student Non-violent Coordinating Committee (SNCC). The success of the sit-ins led to the revival of another method of direct action, first used in 1948 by the Congress of Racial Equality (CORE): the freedom ride. In December 1960 the Supreme Court had declared racial segregation illegal on all interstate buses and trains and at transportation terminals. Under the direction of James Farmer, CORE sent 13 black and white 'freedom riders' into the South in May 1961. Their journey was marked by horrendous violence:

> ...they were assaulted in Rock Hill, South Carolina. White mobs in Anniston, Alabama, attacked and burned one bus. In Montgomery, white racists pulled freedom riders off the bus and administered a brutal beating...in Mississippi freedom riders were given 67-day jail sentences for sitting in the 'whites only' section of the city's bus depot.

M. Marable: *Race, Reform and Rebellion*, 1984

Above: *freedom riders guarded by troops, 1960.*

Right: *freedom riders being arrested in Montgomery, Alabama, in 1961.*

Black and white freedom riders. James Peck, a veteran of the 1948 freedom ride, was severely beaten in 1961.

The cost of these actions in terms of physical injury and suffering was high, but the young people involved had set off a mass revolt which was not going to be calmed until blacks achieved some real progress in civil rights:

> *The civil rights struggle witnessed the most successful application of civil disobedience in the nation's history.*
>
> R. Polenberg: *One Nation Divisible*, 1980

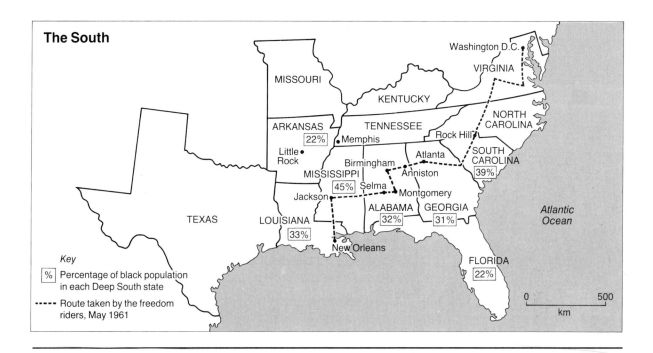

**The South**

MISSOURI

VIRGINIA

Washington D.C.

KENTUCKY

ARKANSAS  22%

TENNESSEE

NORTH CAROLINA

Memphis

Rock Hill

Little Rock

Atlanta

Birmingham

SOUTH CAROLINA  39%

MISSISSIPPI  45%

Anniston

Selma

Jackson

Montgomery

ALABAMA  32%

GEORGIA  31%

Atlantic Ocean

TEXAS

LOUISIANA  33%

New Orleans

FLORIDA  22%

Key

%  Percentage of black population in each Deep South state

----  Route taken by the freedom riders, May 1961

0     500
km

---

*Using the evidence: sit-ins and freedom rides*

A

*Jim Zweig, a white freedom rider, in Montgomery, Alabama.*

*Freedom riders' bus set on fire by whites in Anniston, Alabama. Twelve freedom riders ended up in hospital.*

B  *The young SNCC workers distinguished themselves by their willingness to defy segregation laws...and to go to jail for their principles. It is very difficult, in retrospect, to comprehend the sheer courage of these black teenagers and young adults.*

M. Marable: *Race, Reform and Rebellion*, 1984

31

C *The sit-ins were productive of most change...it was morally wrong, and it was preposterous, that a customer in a store was permitted to buy anything on sale, but if he were colored he could not buy food or drink. No argument in a court could have dramatized the immorality of such a custom as did the sit-ins....*

Ralph McGill (white southern editor of the *Atlanta Constitution*) in his book *The South and the Southerner*, 1964

D *The second thing that grew out of the sit-ins was the use of the economic boycott by Negroes...they spend $7 million a year in Nashville, Tennessee. Shortly before Easter, 1960, 98 per cent of Nashville's Negroes simply quit buying....merchants had not responded to the student sit-ins....*

Louis Lomax: *The Negro Revolt*, 1962

E *The NAACP and the Urban League were the most conservative of the Big Five....now with Negro demonstrations breaking the tranquillity of a hundred cities, law enforcement had acquired a different [meaning], and impatient members of CORE, SCLC and SNCC chided the NAACP on its moderation.*

B. Muse: *The American Negro Revolution*, 1968

1 Would you consider that the two pictures (source **A**) support the statement of the historian, Marable, in source **B**? Explain your answer.

2 How do you think southern readers of McGill's newspaper might react to his statement in source **C**?

3 Explain why, according to sources **C**, **D** and **E**, the sit-ins and freedom rides were so important to the development of the civil rights movement.

## Attacking segregation at its heart

It was essential to keep up the momentum for change created by the events of 1960–61 and to keep public attention across the nation focused on civil rights:

> *...the movement coincided with the emergence of television as the chief source from which Americans obtained the news....stirring, absorbing and easily grasped, civil rights demonstrations...were particularly suited for television coverage.*

> R. Polenberg: *One Nation Divisible*, 1980

Events in Mississippi and Alabama between 1962 and 1963 provide a perfect illustration of this. Mississippi, in the Deep South, was described in 1963 as a 'closed society' based on a belief in white supremacy. Over 40 per cent of the population was black, but:

> *The Mississippi Negro did not vote, did not serve on juries, held no ...office in local government. He attended inferior schools, lived in slum housing, received unequal treatment in the courts, sat in the back of the bus....*
>
> James Silver: *Mississippi; A Closed Society*, 1964

Violence was frequently used to keep blacks in their place. Here are just a few examples:

| Victim | 'Offence' | Result |
|---|---|---|
| Emmett Till, 14 years old. | Wolf-whistled at a white woman. | Mutilated and murdered. Murderers known, tried and acquitted. 1955. |
| Rev. George Lee and Lemar Smith. | Attempting to register black voters. | Shot dead – no trial of alleged murderers. 1955. |
| Gus Courts, 66-year-old black grocer. | Attempted to register as a voter. | Driven out of business, shot and badly wounded. He survived and moved to Chicago. No trial of attackers. 1955. |
| Medgar Evers, NAACP official. | Leader of civil rights activities in Mississippi. | Murdered outside his home. Suspect tried twice by all-white juries; no verdict reached in either case. Suspect released. 1963. |
| Michael Schwerner and Andrew Goodman (both young whites from New York); James Chaney (black). | Working in Mississippi to help blacks gain the right to vote. | Murdered; bodies found six weeks later buried in earth dam. Murderers known but no action taken in 1964. (Tried and convicted in 1967.) |

---

*Using the evidence: the murders of Schwerner, Goodman and Chaney*

A  *[On 21 June 1964] three young men had driven to the town of Lawndale to investigate the burning of a black church there. Around 3 p.m. their blue Ford station wagon was stopped by Deputy Sheriff Cecil Price near the town of Philadelphia, Mississippi. The three were taken to jail in*

*Martin Luther King speaking about the three civil rights workers murdered in Mississippi in 1964.*

*connection with speeding charges, but released later that night. [They were then murdered.] It was not until December that the FBI made any arrests....taken into custody were 21 Mississippians, including Deputy Sheriff Cecil Price....the charges against the men were subsequently dropped in the state court. [Price and six others were found guilty of conspiracy to murder in 1967.]*

J. Williams: *Eyes on the Prize*, 1987

**B** *Everybody knew that at least one of these young people coming to Mississippi was going to be murdered....once the bodies are found, then there is a great...cry to put somebody in jail. That power doesn't exist in Mississippi. There is no way in the world, in open court, where a twelve man jury must be unanimous, and where every juror can...be made to say how he voted — there's no way to ever put anybody in jail.*

A citizen of Philadelphia quoted in W.B. Huie's book,
*Three Lives for Mississippi*, 1965

1 Look again at the evidence in source **A**. Later it was suggested that the arrest and release at night of the three men was part of a conspiracy to murder them. Try to reconstruct the crime from this evidence.

2 Using sources **A** and **B**, explain why so many murders went unpunished in Mississippi.

The increase in racial violence in Mississippi reflected the growing pressure of the civil rights movement. In September 1962 the courts ordered that a black student, James Meredith, should be admitted to the all-white University of Mississippi. The Governor of Mississippi, Ross Barnett, immediately denounced the decision as:

> ...the greatest crisis since the War between the States [the Civil War]....we must stand up like men and tell them 'Never'.

Barnett knew that President Kennedy was determined to support the court's decision. In a private telephone conversation with Kennedy, Barnett agreed that Meredith should be quietly allowed into the university. This was done and Meredith, protected by a force of federal marshals, arrived on the campus. In public, however, Barnett had to appear tough. On television he announced Meredith's arrival, but added remarks that inflamed white opposition. The result was a night of rioting; the campus became a battlefield, with the federal marshals outnumbered. When news of the battle reached Kennedy at 3.55 a.m., he ordered federal troops to move into the university. By morning, two people had been killed, 168 marshals injured and 200 protesters arrested. Meredith completed his course and became the first black to graduate at the university. He later said:

> Some supposedly responsible newspaper men asked me if I thought attending the university was worth all this death and destruction. That really annoyed me....I didn't want that sort of thing...but I know one thing — in the past the Negro has not been allowed to receive the education he needs. If this is the way it must be accomplished...then it is not too high a price to pay.
>
> J. Meredith quoted in T.R. Frazier's book, *Afro-American History*, 1971

Above: *demonstrating for CORE. In the early 1960s CORE (and SNCC) members were mostly young and both black and white.*

Right: *the leaders of the main black organisations meet in 1963. Left to right: John Lewis (SNCC); Whitney Young (National Urban League); A. Philip Randolph (Negro American Labor Council); Rev. Martin Luther King (SCLC); James Farmer (CORE); Roy Wilkins (NAACP).*

In 1963 the growing crisis in race relations came to a head in Birmingham, Alabama. A local church leader invited Martin Luther King to make the city the target for his next offensive. King agreed. Birmingham, he believed, was 'probably the most thoroughly segregated city in the United States'. The Governor of Alabama, George Wallace, and the police chief in Birmingham, Eugene 'Bull' Connor, were well known for their racialist views. When he was elected in 1962 Wallace declared: 'Segregation now, segregation tomorrow, segregation forever.'

Above: *police turn fire hoses on blacks demonstrating in Birmingham, Alabama, in 1963.*

Right: *a demonstrator is arrested in Birmingham, Alabama. Why do you think scenes like these led President Kennedy to propose a civil rights bill in 1963?*

In response to black marches calling for an end to segregation in public places and in employment, 'Bull' Connor's police force reacted with violent arrests. Nationwide television carried scenes of police using fire hoses, electric cattle prods and snarling dogs to break up the demonstrations. Along with other civil rights leaders, King was jailed (for the thirteenth time since the mid-fifties). President Kennedy sent a mediator to Birmingham and eventually an agreement was made with the more moderate whites to begin desegregation. However, the terrible scenes of violence in Birmingham had a much wider importance as they at last moved the federal government to take action and propose a wide-ranging civil rights bill.

Until he acted in 1963, President Kennedy had moved with extreme caution on civil rights issues. In the 1960 election he had won a large majority of black votes. Martin Luther King had been jailed during the election campaign and Kennedy made a much publicised telephone call expressing his sympathy to King's wife, Coretta. Once in office, however, Kennedy disappointed blacks. He may have appointed some to important government posts and encouraged blacks in the South to register to vote, but he avoided introducing a civil rights bill because he did not wish to upset his southern white supporters in Congress. The events in Birmingham, Alabama, however:

> ...awoke the Kennedy Administration from a two-year period of hibernation.
>
> R. Polenberg: *One Nation Divisible*, 1980

To maintain the pressure on Kennedy's administration, black leaders organised a massive march on the nation's capital. On 28 August 1963, 200 000 people (including about 30 000 whites) took part in the march on Washington. Totally peaceful, the marchers sang the anthem of the civil rights movement, 'We Shall Overcome', and at the end of

*The march on Washington, 1963.*

the march listened to Martin Luther King's greatest speech which finished with these words:

> *I have a dream that one day this nation will rise up and live out the true meaning of its creed: 'We hold these truths to be self-evident, that all men are created equal....'*
>
> *I have a dream that one day on the red hills of Georgia the sons of former slaves and the sons of former slaveholders will be able to sit down together at the table of brotherhood.*
>
> *I have a dream that one day even the state of Mississippi, a state sweltering with the people's injustice, sweltering with the heat of oppression, will be transformed into an oasis of freedom and justice.*
>
> *I have a dream that my four little children will one day live in a nation where they will not be judged by the color of their skin, but by the content of their character.*
>
> *This is our hope. This is the faith that I go back to the South with. With this faith we will be able to hew out of the mountain of despair a stone of hope.*

The gulf between King's 'dream' and reality was brought home horrifically in October 1963: while Congress stalled on Kennedy's bill, a church in Birmingham, Alabama, was bombed and four little black girls killed. A month later, President Kennedy was assassinated in Dallas and Lyndon Johnson became President. A southerner from Texas, Johnson was determined to show that he was a liberal in race relations and was prepared to meet opposition in Congress head on.

*Martin Luther King and his wife Coretta celebrating Dr King's award of the Nobel Peace Prize, 1964.*

In 1964, the Civil Rights Act was passed:

| Main terms of the Civil Rights Act, 1964 | |
|---|---|
| 1 | Racial discrimination in public places such as restaurants, hotels and theatres was banned. |
| 2 | Powers were given to the Attorney General (the government's chief legal officer) to ban segregation in schools, libraries, museums and hospitals. |
| 3 | Funds were to be withheld from any projects financed by the federal government if they failed to desegregate. |
| 4 | Employers and trade unions were to end discrimination in employment. |

This wide-ranging Act had one serious omission: it failed to protect the voting rights of blacks. Martin Luther King was determined to follow up previous successes and in 1965 led a campaign for the registration of black voters in Selma, Alabama. King was at the height of his influence and in October 1964 had been awarded the Nobel Peace Prize. At Selma, all the ingredients for King's style of protest were present: a clear issue over the right to vote; a tough racialist sheriff, Jim Clark, quickly seen as the 'villain' of the piece; massive arrests and beatings, all immediately relayed by television to the watching nation. Lyndon Johnson reacted immediately with a bill in Congress. He said:

> ...in Selma...long-suffering men and women peacefully protested the denial of their rights as Americans....every American citizen must have an equal right to vote. We must overcome the crippling legacy of bigotry and injustice. And we shall overcome.

From a speech given by Lyndon Johnson in March 1965

*bigotry:* blindness to anyone else's point of view

*Demonstration by whites against Martin Luther King, Detroit, 1965. How were these demonstrators trying to make King unpopular with white Americans and why do you think they chose this way of doing so?*

*The march from Selma to Montgomery, Alabama, to secure the right to vote, 1965.*

In August 1965 the Voting Rights Act put an end to the various schemes by which blacks had been denied the vote, and, most important, sent federal government officials to ensure fair enrolment of voters. The Acts of 1964 and 1965 were great victories for the black civil rights movement but they were by no means the end of the story.

---

*Using the evidence: Civil Rights Acts, 1964 and 1965*

A *[The Civil Rights Act (1964) went] virtually as far as the law can reach to end the Negro's lot as a second-class citizen.*
*Newsweek magazine, 1964*

B *The Voting Rights Act is one of the most monumental laws in the entire history of American freedom....to-day the Negro story and the American story fuse and blend.*
*President Lyndon Johnson speaking in 1965. Quoted in R. Polenberg's book, One Nation Divisible, 1980*

*discrimination:* acting against the interests of people on the grounds of race

C *The Civil Rights Act (1964)...still left much ground to be covered. It had no provisions, for instance, to protect Negroes and civil rights workers from racist violence in the South...[it failed] to attack the problem of discrimination in housing. Nevertheless, against a long background of unwillingness to face the problem of the Negro's inferior status in the US, the act was revolutionary and it went very far indeed.*
*B. Muse: The American Negro Revolution, 1968*

D  *With powerful new laws on the books, with public sentiment behind them and an administration thoroughly committed to the cause, a new era of progress was about to dawn.*
   C. Vann Woodward (white historian): *The Strange Career of Jim Crow*, 1974

*sharecroppers:* poor tenant farmers

*franchise:* the right to vote

E  *Jim Crow was legally finished, yet black workers and sharecroppers were still the victims of bombs, lynchings ....white liberals were demanding that the Negro 'quiet down' and 'accept' the gains he/she had made. Black Southerners had the electoral franchise; but what of economic security, housing, childcare, medical care and the right to live without fear?*
   M. Marable (black historian): *Race, Reform and Rebellion*, 1984

F  Percentage of voting-age blacks listed in the voting registers of some southern states:

| State | 1964 | 1968 |
|---|---|---|
| Alabama | 14 | 56 |
| Florida | 26 | 62 |
| Georgia | 22 | 56 |
| Mississippi | 4 | 59 |
| South Carolina | 11 | 56 |

1  Why do you think sources **A** and **B** were so enthusiastic about the civil rights legislation of 1964−5?

2  Look again at sources **C**, **D** and **E**, then put each source into one of the following categories:
   a) very much in favour of the legislation;
   b) very critical;
   c) very balanced.
   Explain your decisions briefly.

3  Does the evidence in source **F** enable you to draw any definite conclusions about the 1965 Voting Act? Explain your answer.

4  If you were writing an account of the civil rights legislation of 1964−5, which of the above sources would you find (a) most useful and (b) least useful? Give reasons for your answers.

# BLACK NATIONALISM AND BLACK POWER: 1965-68

In Las Vegas on 22 November 1965 Muhammad Ali, the world heavyweight boxing champion, faced as his challenger Floyd Patterson, another black fighter who was attempting to recover the world title for the third time. Taller, heavier and faster than his opponent, Ali boxed superbly, delivering a torrent of punches which reduced Patterson to battered defeat over 12 rounds. Writing later of the fight, a black nationalist leader said:

> *Muhammad Ali is the first 'free' black champion ever to confront white America. In the context of boxing, he is a genuine revolutionary, the black Fidel Castro of boxing . . . . for there to be such an uproar over Muhammad Ali should indicate that there is something much more serious than a boxing title at stake . . . .*
>
> Eldridge Cleaver: *Soul on Ice*, 1969

The reason for Cleaver's enthusiasm for Ali helps to explain the growth of black nationalist feelings in the 1960s — feelings of a real and separate identity among black people. There had been many

*Muhammad Ali (left), a heavyweight champion with a liking for verse:*
*You've had us in your lock, tight as a cage,*
*and now you're acting shocked, we're in a rage.*
*Us on the bottom with you on the top,*
*That's a game we aim to stop.*
*That's all over now, Mighty Whitey.*
*That's all over now.*
    Muhammad Ali, 1970

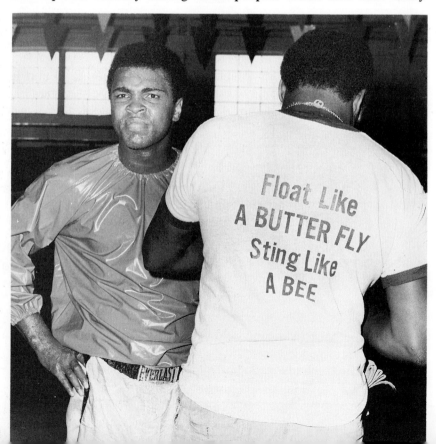

great black boxing champions before Ali; along with some other sports it was one of the few areas of life in which black Americans could compete on equal terms with whites. Ali, however, was different. Most former champions, such as Patterson or Liston, from whom Ali had taken the world title in 1964, had steered clear of politics and avoided upsetting white people:

> *...there is no doubt that white America will accept a black champion, applaud and reward him, as long as there is no 'white hope' in sight. But what white America demands in her black champion is a brilliant powerful body and a dull, bestial mind — a tiger in the ring and a pussycat outside it....*
>
> Eldridge Cleaver, as above

In contrast, Ali had joined the Black Muslims, publicly announcing he had done so by following Muslim practice and changing his name; originally he had been known to the world as Cassius Clay. As the novelist James Baldwin remarked:

*chattel:* slave

> *[It is] a fact that every American Negro bears a name that originally belonged to the white man whose chattel [his ancestor had been].*
>
> J. Baldwin: *The Fire Next Time,* 1963

The Muslims were unpopular with most whites and many moderate blacks. They rejected the idea of the integration of blacks into a white-dominated society, and called for a separate black state. As more blacks were drawn into political activity in the 1960s, the

*Muhammad Ali addressing a Black Muslim meeting in 1968. Why do you think he was unpopular with many white people?*

Demonstration by Black Muslims, 1963.

Black Muslim supporter in uniform.

Muslims grew in number. They were particularly successful in recruiting poor blacks from the city ghettos and in reforming black criminals:

> ...by 1962 over 600 convicts had become converted to the Muslims and were transformed into clean, courteous, hard-working members of their own exclusive communities.
>
> Mary Ellison: *The Black Experience*, 1974

In 1966 Ali became even more unpopular with many whites when he refused to be drafted into the Army for possible service in Vietnam. He was stripped of his heavyweight title and banned from boxing in the United States. Eventually, after a series of appeals through the courts, Ali returned to the ring to regain his title in 1974.

## Malcolm X

To some black leaders the methods of Martin Luther King had always seemed too moderate and his aim of winning concessions from the white majority appeared too limited. Non-violence seemed too often one sided, as blacks were beaten and even killed.

---

*Using the evidence: a black nationalist leader protests*

> They used to sing 'I love everybody' as they ducked bricks and bottles. Now they sing:
> Too much love,
> Too much love,
> Nothing kills a nigger like
> Too much love.
>
> Julius Lester: *Look Out Whitey, Black Power's Gon' Get Your Mama*, 1968

What do you think Lester is saying in this passage?

---

Malcolm X, 1963.

More rebellious voices were heard, demanding respect and equality for black people. One such voice was that of Malcolm X. Born Malcolm Little in 1925, he became a small-time criminal in the black ghettos of Boston and New York, ending up in jail. Reformed by the Black Muslims, he changed his name and rose to become second-in-command to the Muslims' leader, Elijah Muhammad. He quarrelled with Muhammad and in 1964 left the Muslims to found an independent movement. In 1965 he was assassinated by Black Muslims. Malcolm's importance was not as an organiser but as a brilliant public speaker.

*[He] was the voice of urban black protest, calling on Negroes to reassert their racial pride and resist the forces of white oppression.*
J. White: *Black Leadership in America*, 1984

Malcolm saw black people as a nation with their own history, their own literature and their own ideas. Rather than integrate into white society, he believed, according to his biographer P. Goldman, that black people 'should control every aspect of the black community'. He drew a parallel between the position of American blacks and those living in Africa, many of whom had recently overthrown their white colonial rulers.

*The Negro revolt [will] merge into the worldwide black revolution ....the so-called revolt will become a real black revolution.... revolutions overturn systems. And there is no system on this earth which has proven itself more corrupt...than this system that in 1964 still colonises 22 million Afro-Americans, still enslaves 22 million Afro-Americans.*
Malcolm X: *The Black Revolution*, 1964

Malcolm spoke the language of the black masses. The more moderate, usually middle-class, black leaders of the main civil rights movements, as well as most white people, found him a disturbing influence.

*[His violent death] led disbelief and anguish to fuse and form a sharp surge of vengeance in black American minds. Blacks in prison, blacks in ghettos, blacks with hope and those who had dieted on despair, yearned to attack the system that had set the scene and caused his death.*
M. Ellison: *The Black Experience*, 1974

## Black Power

Many of Malcolm X's ideas inspired the more revolutionary leaders who began to appear in black movements in the mid-1960s. These leaders followed Malcolm in being more hostile to white people,

Stokely Carmichael addressing a rally in Los Angeles in 1966. He invented the slogan 'Black Power'.

more prepared to meet violence with violence and less ready to wait for gradual improvements. They also found a new slogan – Black Power. The term first came to national attention during a freedom march led by James Meredith in June 1966. Soon after the march began Meredith was shot and wounded. Among the leaders who re-started the march were Martin Luther King and Stokely Carmichael of the SNCC. Released after arrest on the march, Carmichael said:

> *This is the twenty-seventh time I have been arrested. I ain't going to jail no more. What we're gonna start saying now is 'Black Power'.*
> S. Carmichael: *Toward Black Liberation*, 1966

Martin Luther King called the slogan 'an unfortunate choice of words'. Another moderate black leader, Roy Wilkins of the NAACP, commented that 'black power means anti-white power' and that this was a form of racialism in reverse. As King and Wilkins feared, newspaper and television journalists seized on the phrase to suggest that extremists were trying to take over the black movement. Carmichael defended the idea of Black Power and denied it meant anti-white violence.

The popularity of the slogan resulted from a growing feeling, especially among young black leaders in CORE and SNCC, that King's non-violent tactics were bringing only very slow progress. These two organisations began to squeeze out their white members and stress the need for blacks to take complete control of their own affairs.

The progress that had been made up to 1965 had raised black hopes enormously, yet the immediate results of the Civil Rights Acts had left the lives of many blacks unchanged. There were also problems as the movement went north. In 1966 Martin Luther King went to live in a poor area of Chicago. He started the Chicago Freedom Movement, which aimed to highlight the housing problem — one of the major areas of discrimination in the North. He led a march into an area where estate agents and white residents had worked together to prevent the sale of houses to any black purchasers. The march was met with the sort of violent white opposition that King had so often encountered in the South. The city authorities agreed to try to prevent the exclusion of blacks from certain areas, but little was achieved. White people remained convinced that the value of their property would decrease if black families moved in:

> *Now, I'm not denying any of the Negroes' rights, but I am saying people can talk about brotherhood all they want till it moves next door. I've put everything I have into my home here and I don't want to lose it to a bunch of do-gooders.*
> A white Chicago resident quoted in A. Lewis's book, *Portrait of a Decade*, 1964

In spite of King's efforts in Chicago, the ghetto continued to grow faster than residential integration. Segregation was not enforced by law as it had been in the South, but it existed all too clearly in many areas of northern life:

> *...the Northern Negro could vote...but this was unimportant to many Negroes in New York and Chicago and Boston....reality was life in a slum, education in ancient schools, a job as a bus boy or no job at all.*
> A. Lewis, as above

In these conditions the slogan 'Black Power' had an attractive ring to it.

---

### Using the evidence

A *Every time you see a white man, think about the devil you're seeing! Think of how it was on your slave foreparents' bloody, sweaty backs that he built this empire that to-day is the richest of all the nations.*
Malcolm X: *Autobiography of Malcolm X*, 1965

B *I endured all that pain, literally burning my flesh...in order to cook my hair until it was limp, to have it look like a white man's hair. I had joined that multitude of Negro men and women...who are so brainwashed into believing that black people are 'inferior' — and white people 'superior' — that they will mutilate their bodies to look 'pretty'.*
Malcolm X, as above

**C** *Black Power means black people coming together to form a political force...that can exercise its strength in the black community instead of letting the job go to the Democratic or Republican parties....Black Power doesn't mean anti-white, violence, separatism or any of the other racist things the press says it means. It's saying 'Look buddy, we're not laying a vote on you unless you lay so many schools, hospitals, playgrounds and jobs on us'.*

Stokely Carmichael: *Life* magazine, 1967

**D**

American athletes Tommy Smith and John Carlos outraged many whites when they gave the Black Power salute on the winners' rostrum at the Mexico City Olympic Games in 1968.

1 Why, in source **A**, does Malcolm X refer to (a) the white man as a 'devil' and (b) slavery, which had been abolished a hundred years before?

2 Look again at source **B**. Explain (a) why the teenage Malcolm 'endured all that pain' and (b) why you think he thought this incident important enough to recount in his autobiography.

3 Look again at source **C**, then write a short paragraph explaining Stokely Carmichael's definition of Black Power.

4 What do you think would be the feelings of (a) white people and (b) black people on seeing source **D** in the newspapers? Explain your answers.

## The revolt of the ghetto

*In Watts and Compton, the black districts of Los Angeles, black men and women took to the streets, attacking and burning white-owned property....the Watts rebellion left $40 million in private*

*Riot in Watts, 1965. A rioter is forced into a police car.*

*Riot in Detroit, 1967. The streets resemble a battlefield.*

*property damage and 34 persons killed. Federal authorities ordered 15,000 state police and National Guardsmen into Detroit...43 residents were killed; 2000 injured; 2700 white-owned ghetto businesses were broken into....*

M. Marable: *Race, Reform and Rebellion*, 1984

The patience of the ghetto dwellers had run out, and there was an explosion of violence in almost every major city in America between 1964 and 1968. The riots took a massive toll: 250 deaths, 10 000 serious injuries and 60 000 arrests. An estimate of the costs ran into hundreds of millions of dollars. Nightly during the long hot summers of these years fires raged, sirens wailed and battles were fought in the streets. In the mornings, with tanks patrolling the streets, the scenes resembled those of cities destroyed by war.

The chaos in the cities came as a great blow to the President, Lyndon Johnson. He had hoped that a mixture of civil rights legislation and social and economic aid, through his 'War on Poverty' programmes, would lead to a peaceful resolution of the race problem. Money was spent on a variety of schemes to help the poor, of whom ghetto blacks made up a large percentage. 'Head Start' provided

49

pre-school education; 'Upward Bound' helped bright slum children go to college; Community Action Programmes encouraged local groups to devise health and housing schemes. In the long run, schemes such as these did help the poor but the money was never sufficient, especially as the Vietnam War absorbed more and more money from 1965. In another sense, the programmes were too late. The pent up feelings of the ghetto poor had reached breaking point.

The 1960s riots, which were mainly directed against white people's property rather than white people, shocked the white communities, most of whom knew nothing of the festering poverty and despair of the ghetto:

> *Middle-class women coming in from suburbia on a rare trip may catch the merest glimpse of the 'other America' on the way to an evening at the theatre, but their children are segregated in suburban schools. The businessman may drive along the fringes of slums in a car or bus....*
>
> Michael Harrington: *The Other America*, 1962

One man who did know those areas only too well was Malcolm X:

*hustlers:* petty criminals

> *[I have] a whole lot of respect for the human combustion that is packed among the hustlers and their young admirers who live in the ghettos where the white man has sealed off the Negro — away from the whites for a hundred years...you name the city. Black social dynamite is in Cleveland, Philadelphia, San Francisco, Los Angeles ...the black man's anger is there, fermenting.*
>
> Malcolm X: *Autobiography of Malcolm X*, 1965

That anger had now boiled over and white politicians, journalists and social investigators searched for reasons. Moderate black leaders deplored the violence, but they understood the pent up frustrations involved. President Johnson set up a National Advisory Commission on Civil Disorders, usually referred to as the Kerner Commission after the name of its chairman, Governor Kerner of Illinois. The central conclusion of this thorough report was not popular with many whites: it threw the blame for the situation upon the white majority.

---

### Using the evidence: the rebellion in the ghettos

A *The causes of the recent racial disorders are imbedded in a massive tangle of issues and circumstances....despite these complexities, certain fundamental matters are clear ....white racism is essentially responsible for the explosive mixture which has been accumulating in our cities since the end of World War II....discrimination and segregation in employment, education and housing have resulted in the continuing exclusion of great numbers of Negroes from the*

*polarization:* division

*benefits of economic progress....to avoid the continuing polarization of the American community...would involve substantially greater federal expenditure than anything now contemplated.*

The Kerner Commission Report, 1968

B *I do not believe that...a majority of the people would vote to support the philosophy of the Kerner Commission Report, that we should give the rioters and the law breakers what they demand and maybe they will quit breaking the law....they must be taught to obey the law.*

Senator Long of Louisiana quoted in J.P. Mitchell's book, *Race Riots in Black and White*, 1970

C *Many public figures have insisted that outside agitators, especially left-wing radicals and black nationalists, incited the riff-raff and thereby provoked the rioting....for most white Americans the 'riff-raff' theory is highly reassuring ...but first-hand descriptions of the riots revealed a great deal of support for the rioters among the non-rioters....a middle-aged Negro woman who ran an art gallery in Los Angeles said: 'I will not take a Molotov cocktail but I am as mad as they [the rioters] are.'*

*Molotov cocktail:* petrol bomb

The Kerner Commission Report, 1968

D *The greatest damage inflicted by the mobs is to the hundreds of thousands of decent, law-abiding Negroes who live in Los Angeles....decent Negroes are not to blame for the Negro mobs.*

*Dallas Morning News*, August 1965

1 What, according to the Kerner Report (source **A**), was the fundamental cause of the race riots between 1964 and 1968? Why were black people excluded from 'the benefits of economic progress' and what does the report suggest is the solution to this problem?

2 Explain why Senator Long (source **B**) believed that most people would disagree with the Kerner Report. Why might you expect Senator Long to be unsympathetic to black people?

3 Look again at source **C**, then explain (a) why most white Americans found the 'riff-raff' theory 'reassuring'; (b) why the report thinks the theory is wrong; and (c) what the middle-aged black woman meant by her remarks.

4 Compare sources **A**–**D**, commenting on their reliability as historical sources.

## The assassination of Martin Luther King

Thirteen years after the Montgomery bus boycott, which had made Martin Luther King famous across America, he returned to the South to lead another campaign in Memphis, Tennessee. On the evening of 3 April 1968, he addressed a black audience. He finished his speech with what afterwards seemed like a premonition of his death:

> *I don't know what will happen now. But it really doesn't matter to me now. Because I've been to the mountain top....I would like to live a long life...but I'm not concerned about that now....I've seen the promised land....I may not get there with you, but I want you to know tonight that we as a people will get to the promised land.*

Martin Luther King quoted in D. Lewis's book, *King*, 1969

At eight minutes past six the next evening, while addressing an audience at his motel, King was shot dead by a white assassin, James Earl Ray. The last three years of Martin Luther King's life illustrated vividly the growing problems of the black movement after the legislative triumphs of 1964–5. As SNCC and CORE rallied to the banner of Black Power, divisions grew within the black organisations. NAACP leaders were worried that white support would be lost, frightened away by Black Power slogans. The boycotts and sit-ins, so effective in the South, were unpopular among whites when they were tried in northern cities. The ghetto riots further alarmed the whites and led to a wave of hostility, sometimes violence, against black protesters – a hostility that came to be called the 'white backlash'.

*Protest in Memphis, 1968. Martin Luther King was assassinated while supporting this protest. Why do you think the black protesters are wearing placards saying 'I am a man'?*

When the racialist Governor of Alabama, George Wallace, ran for the presidency in 1968, he won many votes in the North as well as in his native South.

Martin Luther King had played an important role in unifying different strands of the black movement. To white liberals, his moderation and support of non-violence had made him the most acceptable leader. In the harsher climate of Black Power and rioting, he appeared to be losing his influence over large sections of the movement. At the same time, King's own ideas were beginning to change. He still maintained his faith in non-violence, but he became critical of white-dominated American capitalism and its failure to respond to the problems of black poverty:

> *For years I labored with the idea of reforming the existing institutions of society, a little change here, a little change there. Now I feel quite differently. I think you've got to have a reconstruction of the entire society, a revolution of values.*
>
> Martin Luther King speaking in 1966. Quoted in
> M. Marable's book, *From the Grass Roots*, 1980

When he died in 1968, plans were almost complete for a Poor People's March on Washington to focus attention on the gross inequalities of the economic system.

*The depression of a black soldier serving in Vietnam. Why did many blacks oppose the war in Vietnam?*

Also in these last years, King began to speak out in clear opposition to the Vietnam War. It was a controversial stance on an issue which divided Americans of all races. It also meant breaking with President Johnson with whom King had worked so closely in 1964–5. Many blacks saw the Vietnam War as a racial conflict – whites against non-whites – and as such not a war in which they should take part. It was also seen as a waste of resources that could have been used in the War on Poverty programme:

> *We are spending all this money for death and destruction, and not nearly enough for life. We've seen no changes in Watts, no structural changes...as a result of the riots.*
>
> Martin Luther King speaking in 1968. Quoted in J. White's
> book, *Black Leadership in America*, 1984

Martin Luther King was the leader most likely to bring fresh unity to the black cause and his death set off a spontaneous wave of riots among outraged blacks of all shades of opinion. One of his younger critics summed up his importance as the most influential black leader in the post-war period:

> *The one man of our race that this country's older generations, the militants and the revolutionaries and the masses of the black people would listen to.*
>
> Stokely Carmichael quoted in C. Carson's book,
> *In Struggle*, 1981

# BEING BLACK IN CONTEMPORARY AMERICA

*Black revolutionaries?*

| The Black Panthers: the story in brief | |
| --- | --- |
| 1966 | Founded by Huey Newton and Bobby Seale in Oakland, San Francisco. Ten point programme, calling for full employment, land, bread, housing, education, clothing, justice and peace; an end to police brutality and the murdering of black people. |
| 1967 | Newton shot by police while being arrested; tried and jailed. |
| 1968 | Eldridge Cleaver, Panther leader, arrested then released. He fled the country in face of re-arrest. |
| 1969 | Federal Bureau of Investigation (FBI) campaign against Panthers. Panther offices attacked and wrecked in California, Michigan, Illinois, Colorado.<br>Fred Hampton, Chairman of Illinois Panthers, shot dead by police while asleep in bed.<br>Twenty-seven Black Panthers killed by police and 749 arrested and jailed. |

*Black Panthers in Oakland, California, demanding the release from prison of their leader, Huey Newton, in 1968.*

The fate of the Black Panthers illustrates the atmosphere of the late 1960s. The violence on the streets during the ghetto riots and anti-Vietnam War demonstrations led many white people to call for more 'law and order'. Such people felt that blacks should be satisfied with the progress they had made. Under President Nixon, law agencies such as the FBI were encouraged to treat black protesters with increasing harshness. The Panthers attracted particular attention because they dressed in a type of uniform and carried guns 'for self-defence' (which was quite legal in many states). Behind this tough outward appearance, the Panthers 'obeyed a strict set of rules that forbad unprovoked aggression', according to the historian Mary Ellison. Their main support came from people in the ghettos where the Panthers organised a programme of free breakfasts for poor children as well as free health services. Their numbers were never great and they hardly represented a threat of revolution.

The Black Panthers were just one of a number of black nationalist groups that arose in the 1960s. The problem facing blacks in the 1970s and 1980s has been the need to bring about a united movement once again. In 1972 a convention was held in Gary, Indiana, to attempt to achieve this and a National Black Political Assembly was set up. The results were disappointing and no strong black political party emerged.

## Using the ballot box

Moderate black leaders called for the use of the new voting rights to gain a stronger voice in national and local politics. As a result, more blacks voted at elections and this tactic had considerable success in terms of the increasing number of black Congressmen, state legislators and mayors and other officials in the cities. The most obvious change was in the South, where blacks gained influential positions even in the states that had previously been most rigorously segregated. One of the most satisfying examples was the election of Charles Evers, brother of the murdered Medgar Evers, as mayor of Fayette, Mississippi. More blacks also appeared in the top ranks of the federal government, as justices in the courts, and in the diplomatic and civil services. A black lawyer, Thurgood Marshall, prominent in the civil rights movement, became a justice in the Supreme Court, and Andrew Young was appointed Ambassador to the United Nations in 1976.

It was, however, one thing to get blacks elected or appointed and quite another to ensure really effective action on behalf of black people generally. At the national level, black leaders had tied their fortunes to the Democratic Party, but between 1968 and 1989 the Democrats were out of office for all but four years. In 1976, a solid black vote helped to put Jimmy Carter, a southerner from Georgia,

*Jesse Jackson campaigning for the presidential nomination in Atlanta, Georgia, 1988.*

in the White House by a very narrow majority. But he proved to be a highly conservative president and blacks became disillusioned with his policies, especially those which were most important to the poor – health, employment and welfare programmes.

> *Black leaders like Jesse Jackson claimed that they had been betrayed and that Carter was practising a policy of 'callous neglect' towards blacks.*
>
> M. Marable: *Race, Reform and Rebellion*, 1984

For the rest of the period after 1968, none of the Republican presidents – Nixon, Ford and Reagan – revealed any real concern over the issue of race. Hopes were raised among blacks in 1984 when, for the first time, a serious black challenger – the Reverend Jesse Jackson – appeared in the race for the presidency. Jackson had worked with Martin Luther King in the 1960s and in 1970 had some success in helping the poor of Chicago. However, although he did well, particularly in 1988, in the primary elections held to select the presidential candidate, he received no real reward. In 1988 he ran a good second to Michael Dukakis but the Democratic Party did not consider him to be a suitable vice-presidential candidate.

At a local level as well, it was difficult for elected black officials to show much progress in areas such as unemployment and housing. A growing number of large cities elected black mayors, arousing great

*Jesse Jackson with Jim Wright (Speaker of the House of Representatives) and Rosa Parks in Atlanta, 1988.*

hopes of better conditions among blacks. However, as whites moved out to the suburbs, and many businesses moved out as well, the amount of money coming in from property taxes declined sharply. Also, the majority of blacks in the inner cities were in need of welfare assistance. Thus the black mayors and councils had fewer resources to satisfy the hopes of those who had elected them to provide better schools and houses. White people still controlled most businesses and industry, and black workers still tended to fill the worst jobs or to be unemployed. The ghettos continued to decay.

---

*Using the evidence: black voting power?*

A  *Blacks rose to elected positions at all levels of government ....their numbers leaped from 100 in 1965 to 1185 in 1969 and by...1975, there were 3503. The major gains were in the 17 states of the South which account for 55 per cent of all black elected officials....It is too early for hymns of praise, however. Blacks are a long way from implementing ...independent political power through the ballot box.... they are by tradition...overwhelmingly committed to the Democrats [and] on many occasions their loyalty has been taken for granted...without more than token recompense.*
T.L. Blair: *Retreat to the Ghetto*, 1977

57

**B** *The family lives in a crowded section of the Bronx [New York]....altogether 27 people in the family [of four generations] are qualified to vote in the US Presidential election on Tuesday of next week, but none of them intends to vote. There is a photograph of Martin Luther King on the wall [but] politics has no place in the family's life....the [television] news devotes 60 seconds to Bush...and the same to Dukakis....closer to home is the Rev. Jesse Jackson...but after losing an exciting primary race to Dukakis, he has disappeared from TV, not even rating a 60-second glimpse....the big day for this [black] family is Tuesday this week, not next week...the first of the month is when the mother's welfare cheque arrives....*

W.J. Weatherby: *The Guardian*, 31 October 1988

**C** *It seems certain that...a dapper 47-year-old lawyer called Ron Brown will become chairman of the Democratic Party. This will be the highest position ever gained by a black in one of the main American parties. The prospect is regarded with dread by many Democrats, though none of them doubts Brown's skill, intelligence and amiability. What they fear is the colour of his skin, and the way white America (which voted 57 per cent for George Bush last year) may see this....'It's a disaster in the making,' said one [Democrat]. 'We can't elect a black president, and we can't elect a president who seems too close to the blacks.' Not surprisingly, this kind of talk infuriates Brown and Jesse Jackson.*

*The Observer*, 29 January 1989

1 What, according to source **A**, are (a) the political gains made by blacks since 1965 and (b) the reasons for their failure to get real national power?

2 Why do you think the black family in source **B** (a) has a picture of Martin Luther King on the wall and (b) does not intend to vote in the 1988 election? Explain your answers.

3 What evidence is there in these three extracts of a real advance in black political power as a result of the civil rights movement?

4 In the 1960s Robert Kennedy, the President's brother, told black leaders that there could be a black president 'in 40 years time'. Do you think it is likely that a black will be president by the year 2000? Give reasons for your answer.

## Blacks in contemporary society

Many of the outward signs of racial discrimination were swept away as a result of the civil rights movement. In the South particularly the changes were clear:

> Blacks can eat in any restaurant and sleep in any motel. They can register and vote. They can go to school with whites. They can sit in front in the bus.
>
> R. Polenberg: *One Nation Divisible*, 1980

Blacks are now taken on in a variety of jobs once almost completely closed to them.

> In the 1970s, blacks made their way in the world of banks, corporations, government agencies and universities. Since 1970 the number of black students has nearly doubled.
>
> R. Polenberg, as above

*'We still have a dream.' Coretta King led another march on Washington, 20 years after her husband had made his most famous speech.*

Black personalities began to play a more prominent and respected role in the media and the arts. Black actors such as Sidney Poitier, Cicely Tyson and the comedian Eddie Murphy had films built around their personalities. In earlier days Hollywood had usually cast black people in minor roles, often as comic figures. The 1970s and 1980s have also seen the emergence of fine black writers, especially women such as Alice Walker, author of *The Color Purple*. But very few black people have any control over the entertainment industry which is still run by white businessmen.

The story of black success remains very limited. Those who have prospered are members of the black middle class — a black 'elite' or privileged group — composed mainly of doctors, lawyers, teachers, bankers and businessmen and women. They make up about 25 per cent of the black population. They have benefited from a policy of 'affirmative action' by which colleges and businesses, encouraged by the government, have brought in more black people to create a better balance of the races. The incomes and lifestyle of this elite are comparable to that of the white middle class. Republican governments have also encouraged black business enterprise, or 'black capitalism'. Many whites who are optimistic about the progress of race relations use the black middle class as their example.

The majority of black people remain in the same social and economic position, however. Rates of unemployment are still significantly higher than those for whites and blacks still fill more of the less-skilled and low-paid jobs when they do find employment. Many still

*Ku Klux Klan still operating. West Palm Beach, Florida, 1979.*

attend all-black schools (almost 50 per cent of schools are still not integrated, and the majority of these have few resources compared to those attended by white students). This is the result of the continuing residential separation of the races. One method used to get round this problem was to bus children from their home districts into other areas, to achieve a balanced mix of the races in the schools, but this became extremely unpopular, especially among whites living in comfortable suburbs.

Many blacks remain trapped in dreadful conditions in the ghettos, where soaring crime rates and drug problems, largely caused by these conditions, are often unfairly seen as the defects of an inferior race. Family structures in the ghetto are often weak, with large numbers of one-parent families. Commentators in the 1980s have noted the development of an 'underclass': young people, with no hope of a job, who become involved in gang warfare and all types of crime. Only a massive government-financed effort to solve such problems seems likely to succeed, but nothing like this seems in prospect at the end of the 1980s.

It is not possible to reach a final verdict on the results of the long fight for civil rights in the post-war era. There have been clear gains for some blacks and a removal of many of the most obvious forms of racial discrimination. It is too soon, however, to suggest that the fight for real equality with the majority of white Americans has been won. It seems likely that the issue of race will continue to be one of the most vexing for American society well into the next century.

*Blacks still protest about the Klan and police hostility. Brotherhood March, 1987.*

*Coursework assignment: civil rights in America, 1945–89*

The tasks set out below are intended to focus the attention of students on a number of key events and personalities in the period covered by this book. They should help students to develop particular skills commonly demanded by GCSE examination boards.

a) **Skill: selection, arrangement and presentation of relevant knowledge**
   (i) The civil rights movement was most active and successful between 1955 and 1965. Draw up a clear timeline showing the main events in the story of civil rights in this period.
   (ii) Select any two of these events and explain, in about 100 words for each example, why these events were significant in the achievement of more equal rights for black people in the United States.

b) **Skill: understanding historical terminology and concepts**
   Choose two terms from the following list: a) segregation; b) racial discrimination; c) non-violent direct action; d) black nationalism; e) Black Power.
   (i) Write a sentence or two defining the terms chosen.
   (ii) Give examples from the period studied to support your definitions, then explain their importance.

c) **Skill: empathy**
   A British journalist working in the United States in 1965 interviews two people in the street in the state of Mississippi about the Civil Rights Acts of 1964–5. One person is white and one is black. Think of three questions the journalist might ask and supply the replies from each of the interviewees.

d) **Skill: analysis of continuity and change**
   Comparing the position of black people in American society in 1945 and 1989, answer the following questions:
   (i) The position of blacks in the South showed most change between 1945 and 1989. Would you agree with this statement? Explain your answer.
   (ii) In America generally, only some black people benefited from the civil rights movement, even by 1989. Do you agree with this statement? Explain your answer.
   (iii) The civil rights movement did lead to political progress for black people, but helped them much less in raising their standard of living. Do you agree with this statement?

# Skills grid

## A  Historical skills

### 1  Using historical evidence

| | U 7 | U 10 | U 14 | U 16 | U 18 | U 20 | U 24 | U 27 | U 32 | U 34 | U 41 | U 44 | U 48 | U 51 | U 58 | C 62 |
|---|---|---|---|---|---|---|---|---|---|---|---|---|---|---|---|---|
| Comprehension of variety of sources | | | | | | | | | | | | | | | | |
| Distinguishing between primary and secondary sources | | | | | | | | | | | | | | | | |
| Extraction of information | | | | | | | | | | | | | | | | |
| Evaluation, recognising  ★ fact v opinion | | | | | | | | | | | | | | | | |
| ★ gaps and inconsistencies | | | | | | | | | | | | | | | | |
| ★ bias | | | | | | | | | | | | | | | | |
| ★ importance of origin and context | | | | | | | | | | | | | | | | |
| Recognition of inference and implication in a source | | | | | | | | | | | | | | | | |
| Comparison of different sources based on relative reliability | | | | | | | | | | | | | | | | |
| Reaching conclusions on basis of this comparison | | | | | | | | | | | | | | | | |
| Judgement and choice between various opinions | | | | | | | | | | | | | | | | |
| Formation of overview and synthesis of one's own opinion | | | | | | | | | | | | | | | | |

### 2  Empathy

| | | |
|---|---|---|
| Understanding events and issues from perspective of people in the past | | |

## B  Historical concepts

| | |
|---|---|
| Cause and consequence | |
| Continuity and change | |
| Similarity and difference | |
| Time, sequence and chronology | |
| Interaction of individual with society | |
| Conflict and consensus | |
| Historical vocabulary and terminology | |

# INDEX